Journaling with
JESUS

How to Draw Closer to God

Carol Round

WestBow
PRESS
A DIVISION OF THOMAS NELSON

Unless otherwise indicated, all scripture quotations cited in this book are from *The Holy Bible, New International Version®, NIV®* Copyright © 1973, 1978, 1984, 2011 by Biblica, Inc.™

Cover design by Cat Rahmeier

WestBow Press books may be ordered through booksellers or by contacting:

WestBow Press
A Division of Thomas Nelson
1663 Liberty Drive
Bloomington, IN 47403
www.westbowpress.com
1-(866) 928-1240

ISBN: 978-1-4497-3661-3 (sc)
ISBN: 978-1-4497-3662-0 (e)

Library of Congress Control Number: 2012900368

Printed in the United States of America

WestBow Press rev. date: 01/24/2012

Contents

To my dear friends,
Charlie Shotsky, Cat Rahmeier,
Clarice Doyle, Dorothy Willman-Cummins,
Mary Lou Peterson, Judy Riley,
Ella Ross, Charlotta Harrison, Sonya King,

and my pastor, *Dr. Ray Crawford,*
from whom I have learned so much:
thank you for your prayers and encouragement!

A special "thank you" also goes to the women who shared
their prayer journaling stories with me:
Jeanne Martin, Cindy Thomas, Jan Standfield,
Alice Benavides, Cheryl Proffit, DeeAnn Stampes,
Michelle Gourd, Ceanne Brunk, Kim Knaust,
Pat Dexter, Clarice Doyle, Ahnawake Dawson,
Susan Rice, Jennifer Kirby and Lynn Morrissey.

Why is it so important that you are with God and God alone on the mountaintop? It's important because it's the place in which you can listen to the voice of the One who calls you the beloved. To pray is to listen to the One who calls you "my beloved daughter," "my beloved son," "my beloved child." To pray is to let that voice speak to the center of your being, to your guts, and let that voice resound in your whole being.

—Henri Nouwen,
renowned priest and author

Foreword

In today's world, many Christians wade no further than the shallows in their relationship with God. Many things keep us from diving into a deeper spiritual reality. Yet we love God and we have an inner hunger to truly experience God's presence.

For centuries, Christians have practiced certain spiritual disciplines as a way of opening themselves to God. Worship, Bible reading, and fellowship are a few of these practices. This book introduces us to another: prayer journaling.

Many saints of old have found prayer journaling to be an excellent tool for living in a healthy relationship with God. How wonderful it is that many sincere Christians today are revisiting the ancient practice of prayer journaling and finding new power for their faith life.

Carol Round writes as one who has a committed faith and a creative soul. She shares so passionately because she has experienced the joy of prayer journaling in her own life. I hope she will encourage you as she has encouraged me. Through this book, she offers us an opportunity to remember the saints of the past and to hear the testimonies of some saints of today. As you read, you'll be encouraged to listen to God, to reflect, and to keep a journal of the journey. Carol will teach you how with a very practical, step-by-step approach.

As a United Methodist pastor, I believe in having a method. It's not enough to wish and hope for a closer walk with the Lord. We need a method for moving in the direction we wish to go. Prayer journaling has proven to be an effective method. And as you journal in prayer, I pray that you will experience the truth of scripture: "Draw near to God, and he will draw near to you" (James 4:8 NRSV).

Dr. Ray Crawford
Pastor, Claremore First United Methodist Church

Preface

I have been keeping a prayer journal for over ten years. My mornings begin with my *Women of Faith Bible*, a devotional, and a journal into which I pour out my heart to the One who knows me better than anyone, my heavenly Father. Through my daily conversations with Him, my journal entries reveal the heart of a woman changed by His grace and love. My life has changed dramatically since I began seeking His presence each morning before my day becomes busy with the distractions of this world. It is my hope that *Journaling with Jesus* will draw you into a closer relationship with your Abba Father. Let your journey begin with Him. You will be surprised when He shows up to meet you each morning.

Introduction

"Let us draw near to God with a sincere heart in full assurance of faith, having our hearts sprinkled to cleanse us from a guilty conscience and having our bodies washed with pure water" (Hebrews 10:22).

Can you imagine what it would be like to sit down and have a one-on-one conversation with your Savior? Can you picture yourself sitting together on a carpet of clover near a small mountain stream? No one is around to interrupt your dialogue. The only sounds are the water as it flows on its course downstream, the occasional rustling of the grass as a forest creature timidly checks out the intrusion in his world, and the call of a bird seeking its mate.

What would you discuss? What questions would you have? What would He ask you? How long would He be able to spend time with you before He had to move on?

One of the hymns I recall from my childhood is "In the Garden" by Charles Austin Miles. The refrain dances through my mind when I think about spending time with Him.

> And He walks with me,
> And He talks with me,
> And He tells me I am His own,
> And the joy we share as we tarry there;
> None other has ever known.

It is a joy to spend time with my Savior. Although I cannot physically walk through the garden or sit by a stream to talk with Him, through prayer journaling I have found a way to draw closer to Him.

I have been keeping a prayer journal for over ten years. When I reread some of my earlier journal entries, my spiritual growth is evident. Many of my prayers were not answered, and in the words of singer Garth Brooks, "Thank God for unanswered prayers."

Journaling has made me more aware of His presence and of what He wants from me. More than anything, my Abba Father wants a personal relationship based on trust. Imagine being able to communicate your hopes, your thoughts, and your feelings more clearly to your heavenly Father. Prayer journaling can do that once you make it a daily habit.

I challenge you to try prayer journaling for forty days and experience a more intimate relationship with your Savior. Once you start, I know you will feel compelled to keep your daily appointment with Him.

What Is Prayer?

"Do not be anxious about anything, but in everything, by prayer and petition, with thanksgiving, present your requests to God." (Philippians 4:6)

Have you ever struggled with your prayer life? Do you think you need eloquent-sounding words to reach your heavenly Father? Do you ever wonder if God really hears your prayers? Do you ever doubt that God loves you?

You are not alone in your thoughts. Even great heroes of the Bible like King David struggled with their prayer lives and their insecurities. Many examples are found in His Word of people who poured out their pain, grief, confusion, anger, bitterness, depression, and sorrow to God. You are not the first to wrestle with your faith, nor will you be the last.

Lamentations 5:19 says, "You, O Lord, remain forever; your throne from generation to generation . . . Turn us back to you, O Lord, and we will be restored; renew our days as of old."

Prayer is not complicated. We make it that way. If after hearing an impressively spoken prayer by another you feel inadequate, join the crowd. Not everyone is gifted orally. However, your private prayers are between you and your heavenly Father and have nothing to do with word choice. It is about the heart connection you have with Him and your willingness to be open and honest with your Abba Father. *Abba* is the Aramaic word for *father,* used by Jesus and Paul to address God in a manner of personal intimacy.

Before we tackle the art of prayer journaling, let's define prayer. How would you define prayer? Here are several definitions I like, and they aren't found in Webster's dictionary.

"Prayer is communicating with God."

"Prayer is sitting quietly in God's presence."

"Prayer is the way to renewal and spiritual life."
—Greek Orthodox Church Archdiocese of America

"Prayer is being honest with God."

"Prayer is an expression of our relationship with God."

"Prayer is the exercise of faith and hope."
—The Christian Apologetics & Research Ministry

"Prayer is not a half-hearted ritual recitation of words; it is an outpouring of the heart."
—Rabbi Irwin Katsof

"Prayer is a personal dialogue with God, a spiritual breathing of the soul, a foretaste of the bliss of God's kingdom."
—Reverend Patrick Comerford

"Prayer is our direct line to heaven."

"Prayer is responding to God."
—*The Book of Common Prayer*

"Prayer is just friendship with God."
—Joyce Meyer

In *Prayer, A Heavenly Invitation,* Max Lucado says, "Prayer is a window that God has placed in the walls of our world. Leave it shut and the world is a cold, dark house. Throw back the curtains and see His light. Open the window and hear His voice. Open the window of prayer and invoke the presence of God into your world."

Invoking the presence of God into your world doesn't mean you can rub a magic lamp and expect Him to answer your prayers immediately or in the way you want them answered. It's about spending time with your heavenly Father because He created you to have a relationship with Him. He yearns to have an intimate connection with you, but He wants you to desire it, too.

In the apostle John's letters, which were written to encourage love for others and obedience to God, he emphasizes the importance of relationships, not only with others, but also with our Lord. In 1 John 4:7-10 (MSG), John writes, "My beloved friends, let us continue to love each other since love comes from God. Everyone who loves is born of God and experiences a relationship with God. The person who refuses to love doesn't know the first thing about God, because God is love—so you can't know Him if you don't love. This is how God showed His love for us: God sent His only Son into the world so we might live through Him. This is the kind of love we are talking about—not that we once upon a time loved God, but that He loved us and sent his Son as a sacrifice to clear away our sins and the damage they've done to our relationship with God."

Do you want to improve your relationship with God? Do you want to connect on a heart level with the One who knows you better than you know yourself? Does the thought of spending time in the presence of your Maker, pouring out your heart to Him, appeal to your weary soul?

Let me ask you some more questions. Ponder these. What does prayer mean to you? How are you responding to God? The way you respond to your heavenly Father's desire to have a relationship with you is the key to your spiritual growth.

Do you desire to grow spiritually? If not, why? Like any relationship worth having, it takes work on both sides. God is willing. Are you?

I've heard many excuses (and have used some of them myself in the past) for not making time for God. Can you relate to any of these reasons for not putting God first in your life?

- My husband and children demand too much of my time.
- I'm trying to hold down a job and juggle all of my responsibilities at home.
- I'm president (vice-president/secretary/treasurer/reporter) of (insert organization or group here) and I am must (insert duties here).
- My church family expects me to volunteer for (insert committees, projects, etc. here).
- I barely have enough time for myself, let alone God.

Let's examine these excuses, especially the final one. I used to be the "Queen of Busy." I was involved in so many activities that I never had time for myself, let alone God. I was so stressed at times that I wasn't always a pleasant person to be around. Then I came to realize the necessity of putting God first at the beginning of my day. When I began working on my relationship with Him, I was able to step back, survey my life, and reassess my priorities. That's when I learned an important word: no.

No, as in "I'm sorry, but I really cannot commit to this project at this time." No, as in "I really can't take on one more task (office, club, etc.)." No, as in "I would really like to help you out, but I'm overwhelmed with so many other things that I would not be able to give my best to this committee." You get the picture. No means just that: no. You don't have to be rude. However, you must have intention in pursuing a relationship with God, even if it means giving up "good" activities.

Jesus says it best in Luke 9:62 (MSG): "No procrastination. No backward looks. You can't put God's kingdom off till tomorrow. Seize the day."

Seizing the day by beginning it with God is one of the best ways I know to stay focused on growing a relationship with Him. Staying centered on that relationship while praying can be challenging, especially if you are not a morning person. Although I am an early riser, I have found myself dozing off sometimes when I bow my head in prayer, especially if I haven't slept well the night before. I have also let my thoughts drift to my to-do list. However, keeping a prayer journal has helped me to stay focused on my relationship with my heavenly Father. With pen in hand, it is much easier to concentrate. It has also helped me to grow spiritually. When I return to reread entries I made when I first started journaling, I can see how God has answered prayers. I also discover how much I have grown. My prayers are now more about Him and less about me.

Journaling your prayers to Him can help change you from knowing about God to experiencing God in a deeper way. One of the most important things to remember about our relationship with God as we journal our prayers is that we write to grow, not to stay the same. And that's what God wants: for us to grow spiritually.

If you truly want to know Him and move His heart, put aside the formulaic prayers that have become a ritual and open your heart to become the person He created you to be. Remember, He is your best friend. He already knows your thoughts, your feelings, your frustrations, your pain, your hopes, your worries, and your dreams. However, He still wants to hear from you through authentic prayer.

Coming to your Abba Father in authentic prayer means you trust Him to help you become more like Christ. Come to prayer believing that God is with you and will build you up. Have confidence in the Lord, knowing He will help you leave behind those things holding you back from being your best.

What are you waiting for? Let's get started.

"There are many things that are essential to arriving at true peace of mind, and one of the most important is faith, which cannot be acquired without prayer."
—John Wooden, UCLA head basketball coach

Recording Our Inner Journey

"Draw near to God and He will draw near to you" (James 4:8 NKJV).

We might think there are not any examples of prayer journaling in the Bible. However, there are numerous instances of people writing down God's activities and commands in obedience, remembrance and accountability.

- Moses wrote on the tablets the words of the covenant: the Ten Commandments.
- Every new King of Israel was told to write down God's law.
- Joshua reminds the people of Israel not to be negatively influenced by unbelievers, but to obey what God had written down.
- Accounts of God's assistance in people's lives were recorded so that future generations would give Him praise.
- John recorded the life of Jesus so others would know the truth about Him and be encouraged by His promises.

When you read the Psalms, you realize that King David's outpourings about God's greatness, His goodness, and His mercy are written prayers to be sung. Many of the Psalms are prayers and supplications to God which the king made in times of trouble. Other psalms contain positive advice, showing God's people the way to true happiness through virtuous living and the fulfillment of His commandments.

Humans have been keeping diaries and journals since paper and writing tools became readily available. We usually associate a diary with a recitation of the day's events and one's reaction to those happenings. Picture a teenage girl who is heartbroken after being dumped by her boyfriend. Although keeping a diary can be beneficial, the difference between a diary and a journal is emphasis and purpose.

In a spiritual journal, we record our inner journeys. Outward events are not important unless they relate to our inner lives. Journaling not only involves keeping track of the journey but also explores who we are and what we are here for: our purpose. Keeping a spiritual journal leads us to learn more about ourselves. It helps us discover the parts of ourselves that have become hazy or been lost.

In my late forties, I began to keep a prayer journal because I was lost. I began to ask myself, "Who am I?" My nest was empty. I no longer felt needed by my sons. One had married, and the other had just started college. I also went through a divorce after my twenty-eight-year marriage ended. I could no longer identify as a wife or a mother. Through journaling, I rediscovered the most important part of myself. I am a daughter of the most high God, a God who cares about me, a God who hears my prayers, and a God who wants a relationship with me.

Since that time more than ten years ago, my life's journey has become driven by intention. Instead of allowing my peers and the whims of passing fancy to lead me, I have set the goal of building a deeper relationship with my heavenly Father. He longs to meet each of us at the heart of who we are and all that we hope to become.

I had no idea of the trials I would face after rededicating my life to Him in the fall of 2001. My journal became a place to record my cries for help as well as the outcomes of many of those times of despair. The pages of my journal helped me find the beauty of God's activity in my life and in the lives of those I love. When my pen flows across the page writing words inspired by the Holy Spirit, I find clarity in my life.

Philippians 4:7 says, "And the peace of God, which transcends all understanding, will guard your hearts and your minds in Christ Jesus." After spending time with my heavenly Father each morning, pouring out my heart to Him in praise and supplication on the written page, I find peace.

James 4:8 says, "Draw near to God and He will draw near to you." Do you want to draw closer to God? By expressing your thoughts, your feelings, and your insights on the pages of a journal, you will be surprised when you discover God in the process. In turn, He will use your journal as an instrument to transform you. Your journal will also become a way of holding yourself accountable to spiritual maturity.

"If a journal answers just one question,
it is 'What is God doing in my life?'"
—Jan Johnson, author of
Enjoying the Presence of God

Journaling as a Spiritual Practice

"Be joyful in hope, patient in affliction, faithful in prayer" (Romans 12:12).

To realize the true benefits of prayer journaling, we must remember that a journal is different from a diary. You might think of writing in a diary like a report; it's all about what is happening in your life. You might record what you had for lunch or who you met that day. A problem at work or school, or something similar might provoke your writing muse.

However, a journal is different; it's a tool for examining your life. It's all about "so what?" and "what now?" Keeping a journal can lead to insight and growth. A prayer journal, then, is a way to keep track of your journey as well as a written record of your reactions to matters of the spirit. It can also help you to develop greater constancy in your prayer life. How can journaling specifically enhance your prayer life and deepen your relationship with God?

- **Consistent journaling can be a spiritual aid to understanding what God is doing in your life. It can clarify your thoughts and bring about new discoveries about yourself. It can also help you discern how God speaks to your heart.**
  For ten years, I've sat down each morning with my Bible, a book of devotions, and my journal, to spend time with my

heavenly Father. This quiet time is God's time, the time I devote to communicating with Him. During our planned meeting, my focus is on Him. After reading scripture and a daily devotion, I pour out my heart to Him in my journal. Whatever is on my mind or weighing heavily on my heart finds its way onto the blank pages. Inked on those pages are also words of affection for His character and His compassion. My words of praise are whispers in His ear just as He speaks softly into my heart.

- **You can trace your spiritual growth by looking back at your entries.**

  Inside a trunk in my bedroom is a cardboard box containing fifteen journals of various types and sizes, from spiral-bound notebooks to hardcover books designed specifically for journaling. Occasionally, I open the trunk and lift the box from within, the box that holds not only past prayers and memories, but also proof that God is working in my life and in me as well as in my loved ones. I am humbled when I read my earliest entries and then fast-forward to the current year. It reaffirms for me that God cares for His children.

- **Keeping a daily prayer journal can assist your understanding of the nature and will of God. However, it requires you to slow down and take time to listen for His voice.**

  When I was considering a job change, writing in my journal and asking God for guidance helped me to make the best choice. Seeing my thoughts on paper brought clarity to a situation that would have been life-changing had I chosen to leave my teaching career before retirement. I didn't. It was nearly six months later that God affirmed my decision to stay had been the right one. I've learned to trust the peace that passes understanding when I am considering a major change in my life. Through writing in my journal, I become more aware of His guidance.

- **When you organize your thoughts in writing, you will have new ideas that may never have occurred to you otherwise. The act of writing your prayers down allows more freedom to express yourself.**

Before my earthly father went to be with the Lord in 2007, I had struggled to come up with a plan that would suit both of our needs. My mother had passed away in 2004. Dad had turned eighty in 2006, and I was concerned about him living alone. I had moved to a new community the previous year. Living more than 100 miles away, round-trip, made it difficult for me to check on him each day other than our morning telephone conversations. I didn't know if my dad's health was okay or if he was just telling me he was fine to prevent me from worrying. One morning, as I was sharing my concerns with God in my journal, a possible solution came to mind. Although it didn't work out, it made me realize the value of taking everything to God in prayer.

- **When you need encouragement, you can look back at the written record of your prayers and see that God is always faithful, even when we aren't. It helps us see God's power displayed in our lives.**

Writing down prayers is one of the most encouraging things you can do in your spiritual journey. When I reread entries where I have asked for specific things and had those prayers answered, I am overwhelmed by His goodness. I was diagnosed with breast cancer in 2002, ten months after my marriage ended. My emotions were still raw from that life-changing event. Writing in my journal helped me to make sense of and to feel peace about the choices I needed to make concerning potential treatments. I was blessed. Other than two lumpectomies, I needed no further treatment.

- **Prayer journaling compels you to take time on a regular basis to communicate with God and to make sense of the craziness in your daily life. Thus, you gain perspective on what is important.**

If spending time with your heavenly Father is a commitment, prayer journaling is the discipline that enables you to bond in a deeper way. Escaping from the cacophony of life—ringing phones and other technology, for example—focuses you on the One who created you. Before beginning your hectic day, seek the Lord in prayer in order to prioritize what is important. By giving Him the first part of your day, you stay focused on His plans for your life while avoiding the demands of the material world. As my relationship with my Abba Father has grown, the things I thought I needed to be happy no longer control my thoughts or actions. I now hunger for more of Him.

- **Keeping a prayer journal guides you to gain deeper insight into who you are, what your potential is, and how to attain it with God's help.**

  For too many years, I was a people-pleaser. I was overly concerned with how others viewed me. I had a hard time saying no when asked to take charge of a project or activity. Many times, I said yes because of my own insecurities. Keeping a journal has allowed me to see myself as God sees me: a beloved daughter who is loved for who she is and not what she does or can do. If not for the extreme makeover He accomplished in me—and I'm still a work-in-progress—you would not be holding this book in your hands.

- **Through journaling, you recognize your own uniqueness and how your spiritual path differs from other people's. God created each of us with different talents and gifts.**

  Before I answered God's call, I was envious of the gifts and talents of others. My talents don't lie in the musical field, nor am I gifted in the business arena. Though I am not athletically inclined, I began to compete in 5K races when I was in my mid-forties, and even won some trophies and medals in my age division. I realized during that time that running wasn't about winning accolades; it was about doing my best. As Paul said in Acts 20:24, "I consider my life worth nothing to me; my only aim is to finish the race and complete the task the Lord Jesus has given me—the task of testifying to the good news of God's grace." Before that, I wasn't aware of God's plan to use my gifts and talents for His glory. Through my daily habit of journaling, He has made me appreciate the importance of letting Him shape and mold me into the woman He created me to be.

- **Documenting your prayers in a journal frees you to be more authentic with God. He knows your heart and thoughts anyway.**

  If you look up the definition of authentic, you will find the following: genuine, real, not fake, reliable, and trustworthy. Now look up the antonyms, or opposites, of these words. You'll find these words: counterfeit, fake, false, unreal, and untruthful. Do any of these words describe your relationships with others? I wasn't true to myself in the past when I agreed to take on projects only because I thought I had to prove myself worthy. With our heavenly Father, you don't have to fake it. You don't have to prove yourself worthy of His love. You just have to accept His wonderful gift of grace.

- **Putting your thoughts to God in writing encourages self-directed growth.**

  What does it mean to be self-directed? If directed means guided, regulated or managed, self-directed means you have chosen to manage yourself, and in the case of prayer journaling, to manage your time so you can spend part of each day with your heavenly Father. You are not bound by rules but by a desire to spend time with Him and to grow your relationship. Because I have all of my tools in the same place, my morning time has become a refuge from the world. It is a sanctuary I look forward to entering, a place where I come to meet God for our one-on-one time without interruption.

- **Journaling allows us to see ourselves as others see us.**

  If you are to be honest with God, you must be honest with yourself. Journaling and pouring out your heart to Him tears down the walls you have built to protect yourself from past hurts, disappointments, and failures. Putting those feelings down on paper opens you up to healing and identifying who you need to forgive, including yourself. Prayer journaling has been a catharsis for me, allowing me to purge the negative emotions of my past and the baggage that came with them.

- **Journaling can be an accountability tool, allowing you to record your promises to God.**

Have you ever made a promise to God? Have you forgotten about it because of life's craziness? I know I have. Use your journal as an accountability tool, not only to record your promises, but also to remind yourself of your commitment to God. He knows and forgives your forgetfulness. Your journal will help you keep your promises.

- **Prayer journaling is putting your feelings and ideas about God and other people into words. It is a way of seeing your feelings.**

  Have you ever had trouble understanding what you were feeling about a particular person or situation? Maybe you thought it was anger, when in fact, it was disappointment. Many times, your emotions can deceive you because of factors you don't recognize. For example, when I'm tired, I'm not as patient with myself or with others. Sometimes, we take for granted our wide array of emotions because we tend to label them with simplified terms, like happy or sad. You might say, for example, "I'm happy," but does that word do justice to your feelings? Might *jubilant, ecstatic,* or *thrilled* better describe your emotions? How can you better express your feelings? By putting your thoughts on paper, you recognize what you are feeling more easily. By being still and examining what is going on inside of yourself, you can better understand your motives and reactions to people, situations, and even to God. You might even be angry with God, which is okay. He understands you better than you understand yourself. Keeping a journal helps you sort out those feelings and develop better relationships with others, as well as your heavenly Father.

- **Journaling relieves stress, heals past hurts, and transforms your life.**

  I am a walking testimony to the healing that God has brought to my life. My baggage was so heavy I suffered from physical pain as well as other health issues. Let me explain. Did you know that when you carry around your past hurts, or allow stress to rule your life, it affects you physically? This is called the mind-body connection. Your body responds to the way you think, feel and act. When you are stressed, anxious, or upset, your body tries to tell you something isn't right. Poor emotional health can also weaken your body's immune system, making you more susceptible to colds and other infections during emotionally difficult times. For many years, my internal baggage affected my body in many ways. A stress-filled marriage and poor self-image led to frequent back pain, a stiff neck and an upset stomach. However, it wasn't until I was diagnosed with breast cancer in 2002 that I learned about this important connection. After my second surgery to make sure all of the cancer cells were gone, I attended counseling sessions at Cancer Treatment Centers of America, where I learned about the mind-body connection. Proverbs 23:7 says, "For as he thinks in his heart, so is he." Putting my thoughts on paper in the form of a letter to the Lord is one of the best ways I have found to let go of stress and let God be in charge. He wants us to come to Him with confidence that He will deliver us. "We can go to God with bold confidence through faith in Christ" (Ephesians 3:12). Hebrews 4:16 says, "Let us come boldly to the throne of our gracious God. There we will receive His mercy, and we will find grace to help us when we need it."

- **Keeping a daily prayer journal reminds you for whom and for what you need to pray. Your journal is also a place to record the things for which you are thankful.** During my college days, I learned and remembered things by writing them down. Keeping a daily prayer journal works in the same way, by helping you remember who needs your prayers and for what you need to pray. Whether it is for family or friends, or for a situation or a problem, your journal is a place to record the names and things for which you need to pray. Have you ever told someone you would lift them up in prayer, but forgotten to do so? I have. However, a journal not only reminds you to do so, but also, when prayers are answered, is a wonderful reminder of God working in your life. Your journal is also the place to thank Him. Thank Him for providing for you. Thank Him for healing you. Thank Him for every good and wonderful thing in your life. But most of all, thank Him for sending His Son to die on the cross at Calvary for us. "For God so loved the world that He gave His only Son, so that everyone who believes in Him will not perish but have eternal life" (John 3:16).

"Prayer is about a conversation with our loving God—not about wearing Him down to get what we want."
—Nancy Guthrie, *Today's Christian Woman*

Women Who Journal Their Prayers

"But I cry to you for help, Lord; in the morning my prayer comes before you" (Psalm 88:13).

Why should you begin keeping a prayer journal? The following women began prayer journaling for different reasons and at different stages in their lives. Persevering with this spiritual discipline has drawn them closer to God. Each of these women, by recording her walk with God, has been able to track her spiritual growth, her maturity. I know that ten years of spiritual journaling has done that for me.

1 Peter 2:2-3 (MSG) tells us that we are like newborn babies who "crave pure spiritual milk."

> You've had a taste of God. Now, like infants at the breast, drink deep of God's pure kindness. Then you'll grow up mature and whole in God, so that by it you may grow up in your salvation, now that you have tasted that the Lord is good.

At the tender age of eight, Jeanne Martin opened her journal and began writing to keep a record of her relationship with her best friend, Jesus. "I was at a Girl's Auxiliary camp in Oklahoma—Camp Nunny Cha-Ha—and at 5:00 p.m. each evening, the campers were given a sheet with a Bible verse and some questions. I discovered I enjoyed writing what I thought about verses and have done it off and on ever since," says Jeanne, who is now in her mid-fifties.

Writing in her journal each day is mandatory for Jeanne. "It has made me conscious of my desire to be nearer today than yesterday," she says. "If I miss a day, it's hard for me to do my best work.

"Journaling has helped me through some very rough times in my life," Jeanne adds. "The Lord has indeed blessed me and I love having those good and sad times chronicled for my family to see. Even if the journals were to perish, just knowing I had recorded them would be good enough for me."

Another woman who began journaling at an early age is Cindy Thomas. To deal with her loneliness, Cindy began putting her thoughts on paper when she was ten. However, it wasn't until about ten years ago, when she accepted the Lord as her Savior, that she began prayer journaling.

"It started a communication with God and that has helped me to listen and harken unto His voice," says Cindy, who believes prayer journaling keeps her grounded and humble. "It holds the secrets and mysteries of my life; desires, fears, prayers, heartaches, victories . . . it lets me know where I've been and sometimes lets me in on where I am going."

For Cindy, it is also a way to keep track of how awe-inspiring God really is. "We need to be reminded of our test so we can be the testimony for others who have gone through the same things."

Cindy also compares keeping a prayer journal to taking photographs. "Scrapbooking is all the rage these days," she says, "but wouldn't you like to know what your thoughts were while you were being photographed? A picture is like a thousand words, but words alone can build up or destroy those around us. Photos don't always portray memories as well as the written word."

I think Cindy has a point, one I had never considered until recently, when I was going through old family portraits with my sister. We discovered photos of our mother that we had never seen—or if we had, we'd forgotten them. As I looked at the grainy black-and-white and sepia-toned pictures of my mother as a young adult, I wondered: What were her thoughts? Did she experience the same doubts and fears that most of us, as women, do? What did she pray about? Did God answer her prayers? Which ones?

I will never know. But women who keep prayer journals are chronicling God's work in their lives, not only for their own benefit but also for those with whom they share the awesome power and love of having a relationship with Him. It is a powerful testimony.

Jan Standfield started writing down her testimony after a born-again experience. "It has been a tremendous blessing over the years to go back and read and see how the Holy Spirit has worked with me and in me to develop my faith in God, in others and in myself."

Jan's journals are filled with "praise reports, tears, happy thoughts, sad ones, hopes, dreams, thanksgiving—these are in between the prayers and letters to my Father," she says. "I will always keep a journal; it allows me to communicate with God and to see how the Holy Spirit is growing me through the events, people and the Word of God that He brings across my path."

Alice Benavides first picked up a pen to journal over thirty years ago. "I realized that if I kept my thoughts and inspirations on paper, I would better recall them," she says. "I could also keep track of my prayers and see God move. Sometimes I realize just what it is that God is telling me as I'm writing. I love those moments. God has spoken something to my heart and I've captured it on paper as best I can." For Alice, this is the rewarding aspect of journaling. "Sometimes the written word doesn't quite nail it down like my heart does, but it's usually good enough to bring it back to memory. I've reread my journals many times," she says. "I find it faith-building."

Alice also has a system for marking answered prayers in her journal. "I write *AP* and circle it by the prayer request."

There is a sense of victory to be had in physically going back and looking at what you have written in your prayer journal, and seeing how God has worked those things out for your good. "I look back and read about going through chemo and radiation, many things I cannot remember," says Cheryl Proffit, who has journaled for over twenty-five years. "But they are written, and I see God's intervention in my life, and I am grateful. Day to day, the acknowledgement of Him is there and He has created a contented life for me."

However, it wasn't always that way for Cheryl. "Why was I so uptight over such small things? I see the distance that God has taken me, and we have covered a lot of ground. I see how He has arranged my life and moved me from situation to situation and event to event, and I believe that I am exactly where He wants me."

Cheryl's written prayers have also provided other revelations. "Those old journals show me how immature and self-centered I walked, and along the journey, many answers to prayers."

A prayer journal was DeeAnn Stampes' way to cope with spousal abuse and eventually, divorce. "It was extremely difficult in the beginning to discipline myself to set aside the time to write. I had a hard time getting my thoughts out of my head and down on paper," she says. "But once I began, everything started to get clearer and my thought process began to change."

DeeAnn is now an avid daily journaller. "There is a huge release to be able to write out what I am thinking." She always begins her quiet time with God by journaling. "I give God my thanks first and praise Him," she explains. "Then I write what I am struggling with in my life or what my children are struggling with. I then read God's word, find scripture that speaks to me, and write it down.

"By doing this, I can go back and meditate on the Word. This is conversation, a relationship with God. I talk, He listens. He talks, I listen."

Like others who keep prayer journals, DeeAnn emphasizes that the process is about building a relationship. "How do you build a relationship with someone? By spending time getting to know one another."

Although DeeAnn readily admits that journaling her prayers was not easy in the beginning, the activity has changed and developed over time. "It didn't come easy or natural for me. But I didn't give it up. I had made the commitment to journal on a daily basis. Now," she says, "I just start to write and I just keep writing."

By rereading past entries, DeeAnn is also able to see and know that God is working in her life and in her children's lives. "I have seen God answer many of my prayers." More importantly though, DeeAnn says that journaling her thoughts, concerns, prayers, and praise to her Lord and Savior has cleared her thought process and allowed God to speak to her.

Another woman who faithfully writes in a prayer journal is Michelle Gourd. Michelle was motivated to embark on this spiritual journey over eight years ago because, she says, "God was doing so many wonderful things in my life and I wanted a way to keep track of them. I call them 'my conversations with Father.' I pray and then I write what comes to my spirit. A lot of the time, I find that He is encouraging and always letting me know that everything is going to be okay."

From her journaling time, Michelle has learned to listen for that still, small voice when she is quiet. "I write down what I am saying to Him and what He says to me. Sometimes I have inspiration and I write for hours about things that God has placed on my spirit or my heart.

"After praying and coming to a place of peace within myself, I began to focus on the now or the moment of my time with Him," she says. "I have also memorized a lot of scripture. Many times I love to just brainstorm and look up verses, just to see if I still remember them."

Remembering what God has done in her and through her is easy when she rereads her journal entries. "I am amazed when I read in them how much the Father has changed me, and also I am shocked at my stubbornness," she admits. "I may spend a solid month bringing the same old thing up, until one day I get a breakthrough and finally figure out what God is trying to teach me."

Prayer journaling has also helped Michelle deal with her daughter's chronic illness. "I have peace in the middle of the turmoil. One thing I have learned through journaling is how to hear the Father, and also how to receive what I need to stop this constant chatter or worry in my mind."

A family illness also motivated Ceanne Brunk to pick up pen and notebook. She began prayer journaling as a way of coping with her father's health issues. More than fifteen years later, that need to express her thoughts to God through writing has become a habit. "I always write at night because there are usually a lot of things I want to pray about, and that is the best time for me. When I write it out and can actually see it, it is more important to me and I know God listens," she says. "I go back and read what I have written a lot. I prayed about a lot of stuff and it is really neat to go back and read to see which ones God has answered."

Keeping track of answered prayers is also the reason Kim Knaust began keeping a journal several years ago. Rereading her journal entries helps Kim remember and grow her faith. "By trusting Him in troubling times, I have come to realize that He is the only One who will never truly fail us. The most rewarding part of keeping a prayer journal has been a closer relationship with the Lord."

For almost sixty years, Pat Dexter's thoughts, fears, prayers and hopes have graced the pages of a notebook. "I have kept a journal since I was a preteen," she says. "Sometimes it has been a regular journal, but it has always included prayers, many of which God did not answer—thank God!"

Pat also affirms that prayer journaling has improved her communication with God. "I have been better able to express myself, and God has become my friend as I have visited with Him. I have always been better able to express myself in writing, and that has been true in praying also, but as I wrote more letters to God, I found I could talk easier also."

Rereading what she has written in previous entries allows Pat to compare how she was thinking then to how she is thinking now. "I like the comparison so I can actually see how far I have come. I also see the answers to prayers. Some are unexpected and come long after the prayer, but I find the request in the journal and am able to see the answer that eventually came," she adds.

Pat's difficult childhood, which involved abuse, made it difficult to get close to her father. "Writing down those things has helped me overcome that fear," she says. "That is why I can now call God 'Abba.' I certainly can see how He changed me."

For former newspaper editor Clarice Doyle, prayer journaling is a way to bring order to the chaos that often fills her days. "I have found focus for my prayers through writing and learned to document specific requests and answers to those requests," she says.

Through journaling, Clarice reaffirmed her faith in God's concern for our daily lives and for the needs of those for whom she prays. "Often we fail to see the hand of God in situations, or downplay the significance of God's work in our daily lives when we have not documented the beginnings or our own needs or requests and followed through to resolution. Sometimes, when I reread what I have written months before, I am surprised to find that God has answered those prayers in the meantime and I failed to notice it, to thank Him for His goodness."

Like many women who journal their prayers, Clarice writes as if she is having a conversation with God. "I tell Him what has happened throughout the day or week, just like I would if my earthly father or mother were here today. Sometimes it's just regular daily meanderings. Other times, I find myself pouring out my heart, working through my anguish over a particular incident or frustration."

A difficult time in Ahnawake Dawson's life twenty years ago led her to begin putting her prayers into writing. "I felt it would help me to focus," says Ahnawake. "My journal helps give me direction. Many times, after reading the Bible, writing down my thoughts helps me to focus after thinking about that particular scripture."

Ahnawake is also one of many women who return to reread earlier journal entries because it allows her to see how some prayers were answered. "If I don't see that they have been answered, I study why. Sometimes they have been answered but maybe not the way I hoped."

Pastor Susan Rice has kept a prayer journal for more than thirty years, but she admits that at times in her life, she was not consistent with journaling. "It may depend on what is going on in my personal life, but I try to do so at least once a week, and some weeks I write every day."

An encounter with an atheist became the motivation for Pastor Susan to begin her prayer journal. "I was in my early twenties when I found myself one day sitting next to an atheist on a bus. He began talking to me about my faith. I walked away from that experience with much remorse that I had not been able to articulate my faith as well as I wanted."

Because of that regret, she decided to study and meditate on God's Word. "I did not want to take a chance on forgetting some of the thoughts that would come to mind," Susan says. "Writing it down seemed to give me the strength to apply my meditation to everyday life."

Susan uses her journal to communicate better with God. "It is like a Listener for me. I am very verbal and often form my thoughts aloud. If they are truly private thoughts or if no one is around to hear, the journal plays that role. I have had many epiphanies while writing in response to God's Word or while working through grief or emotional pain."

While she does not make a regular habit of returning to the pages of her journal to reread what she has written, Susan does go back to find things she can use as illustrations for sermons or other teaching experiences. "Still other times I will go back to remind myself of promises that I had either made to God or myself, or to remember what God has spoken to me in the past about an issue that I am working on. It is very encouraging."

Pastor Susan likes to urge others to begin writing in journals. "It is a very rewarding experience. It can help you map out your spiritual journey and serve as an accountability measure. It is very humbling to pull out a journal written several years earlier and realize you are still struggling with the same issue."

I am sure that if she met that atheist on the bus today, Pastor Susan would not have any trouble articulating her beliefs. "Keeping a prayer journal has helped me to own and articulate my faith," she says.

Much like Pastor Susan, Jennifer Kirby has discovered that keeping a prayer journal guides her in becoming "a doer of the Word and not just a reader or a hearer."

Although some women journal their prayers every day, Jennifer finds that writing once a week is beneficial for understanding scriptures, applying them, and praying over them. She doesn't always journal during her devotions time, but does so whenever she wants to spend a longer time with the Word and doesn't have time constraints.

For those who have never kept a prayer journal, Jennifer offers a method she calls the SOAP approach. "Don't just read scriptures but write about them," she says.

Read the **<u>S</u>criptures**.
Write an **<u>O</u>verview**.
Write how you will **<u>A</u>pply** it to your life.
Write a **<u>P</u>rayer** that focuses your life on accomplishing what God has shown you.

Like these faithful women, I have discovered the power of journaling as a spiritual aid to know my Creator more intimately and to better understand His perfect plan for my life. Wouldn't you like to do the same?

Letters to God

A conversation with author and prayer journaler
Lynn Morrissey

Lynn Morrissey is an author, speaker, and communicator who specializes in creating programs for Christian women. Her book *Love Letters to God: Deeper Intimacy through Written Prayer* has received outstanding reviews. She is also the author of *Seasons of a Woman's Heart* and *Treasures of a Woman's Heart* and is a contributing author to numerous best-selling anthologies, magazines and newspapers in the Christian press.

Q. When and why did you start keeping a prayer journal?

I began journaling over thirty years ago in a crisis situation, which is often how people start. A woman at work was bent on getting me fired and sabotaged me by lying to my boss. Out of frustration, every day I'd leave my office for lunch and take my day planner, where I began pouring out my frustrations in writing. I'd write, write, write, vent, vent, vent, and before I knew it, I was crying out to God: "Dear God, she did this . . . and Dear God, she did that . . . and Dear God, what am I going to do?"

I was praying without even realizing it! I was talking to God in my own words, my own way, about a real-life situation. Before that, I had been extremely awkward at oral prayer. I didn't know what to say or how to say it.

I tried emulating the flowery prayers of pastors and the expressive prayers of friends, but I always fell short and my prayers trailed off into oblivion, unexpressed. Sometimes I would even fall asleep when I attempted to pray. I loved God and read His Word daily, but I realized something significant was missing from our relationship. I know now that the missing ingredient was prayer.

But, as impossible as this may sound, as a Christian, I just didn't know how to pray. Yet when I picked up my pen, absolutely everything changed. Writing to God freed me. I, who had stopped praying, suddenly couldn't stop praying. I, who could barely utter two sentences to God orally, could now journal for even as many as four hours consecutively. This was nothing short of miraculous. I have been journaling ever since and have countless stacks of journals—written records of my word-for-word conversations with God—that document our relationship. Let me also distinguish that, for me, a prayer journal is not a list of requests, dates, and answers. My journals are my actual, verbatim prayers to the Lord, what I call my "love letters to God," in which I express all my emotions and concerns. They're not pious, lofty or flowery. True love expresses *all* emotions, the good, the bad, the ugly; and true love—God's true love for me—accepts them.

Q. How has journaling transformed your relationship with God?

Since I began journaling, my relationship with God has been absolutely revolutionized. Because I can now write freely, I never run out of things to say to God. I am no longer a prayerless Christian. And because I spend far more time in His presence, my life has dramatically changed. In fact, you just can't spend that kind of time in God's presence and not change. Through reading His Word and journaling unto Him daily, the Lord has healed me from suicidal depression, alcoholism, the pain from an abortion, jealousy, anger, bitterness, complaining and worry.

Most of all, He has transformed me from a prayerless, powerless, purposeless Christian, into one who loves Him and regularly and intimately communicates with Him, one truly changed by His power, and one who knows her God-given purpose and lives it out. My purpose is to encourage transparency through journaling and journaling classes. And now, by living my purpose, it is my great privilege to see and facilitate change in others.

Q. How else do you achieve your purpose?

I have written one book about prayer-journaling called *Love Letters to God: Deeper Intimacy through Written Prayer*. I have also written a self-published study guide to accompany it, and I have an idea for another journaling book. Currently I am studying to earn a credential in journal facilitation, a CJF (Certified Journal Facilitator), with The Center for Journal Therapy in Denver. I have written curricula for several journal courses as part of this credentialing process.

Treasures in God's Word

"For where your treasure is, there your heart will be also"
(Luke 12:34).

One morning, it happens. You stare at the blank page. You can't think of what to say or how to pray. Your spirit is empty. It happens to all of us. We are stuck. I don't call it writer's block but a spiritual block. One solution is to pray through a passage of scripture.

When we use His truth, God has an opportunity to shape us by molding our thoughts to be in agreement with His thoughts. The Psalms are a rich source of inspiration because of the variety of human emotions expressed in its 150 chapters. Guilt, anger, fear, joy, sorrow, desperation, vengeance, praise, peace and, of course, thankfulness, run the gamut of our humanity. Most of us have experienced these emotions at one time or another in our own lives. From this book of poetry and prayer, we read how the psalmists responded to God honestly, devoutly and faithfully and we can learn from their written examples. The Book of Psalms is the best expression of the heart of prayer.

The psalmists had no trouble pouring out their hearts to God. When we read and acknowledge the messages in the Psalms, we are also responding to God. One way to do this is to pray through the Psalms. Choose one. Read it, savor it and ask yourself which verse or verses are speaking to you at this time in your life. Copy the verse or verses down in your journal and begin to meditate on the words. What does it mean to you? How is God speaking to you through the ancient words that are still relevant today?

The last sentence of Psalm 2 reads, "Blessed are all who take refuge in him." I can relate when reading this passage, especially through trials when I wanted to run away instead of seeking God's safe haven. Even though King David wrote these words thousands of years ago, we can still understand the human need for comfort. Although we might want to escape physically from our troubles, when we take refuge in our heavenly Father, we are placing our trust in Him. He is our sanctuary.

I think that is one reason that keeping a spiritual journal is so powerful. In the process of writing, we can also more honestly admit our need for Him. When we come into His presence and bare our souls on the page, our words reflect a desire to know and to be known by our Creator.

On the roller coaster of life, we will experience many emotions. During the good times too, we can find verses to reflect our hearts full of thanksgiving and celebration.

> We wait in hope for the Lord;
>   he is our help and our shield.
> In him our hearts rejoice,
>   for we trust in his holy name.
> May your unfailing love be with us, Lord,
>   even as we put our hope in you.
>   —Psalm 33:20-22

While I usually have no trouble pouring out my heart in praise for all He has done in my life, words sometimes seem inadequate and all I can say is, "Thank you, Father."

If troubles have left you seeing the glass as half empty, consider the following questions to lift your spirits and to help you see God's grace at work in your life.

- **For what or for whom can I be thankful today?**
  Maybe it's just the fact that your car is running smoothly or someone let you go ahead of him or her in the grocery store checkout line.
- **What has God done in my life recently or even in the past?**

Sometimes we look for a confetti moment, when it is the small things each day we overlook and take for granted. When we are open to Him and His presence in our daily lives, we begin to recognize the moments when He is speaking to us. For example, on a recent morning walk, a hawk flew lazily overhead. I was not particularly excited about my day until I saw the bird and felt it was God's way of saying to me, "See my creation and know that you are a part of it." I promptly said, "Thank you, God for your beautiful creation."

- **What lesson have I learned recently through personal experience, or another person's, that I can use to help others?**

When we start looking at ways to help others, our troubles seem to diminish. In 2 Corinthians 1:3-4, the apostle Paul writes, "Praise be to the God and Father of our Lord Jesus Christ, the Father of compassion and the God of all comfort, who comforts us in all our troubles, so that we can comfort those in any trouble with the comfort we ourselves receive from God."

Don't let the blank page syndrome intimidate you. Writing is like any endeavor in life; the more you do it, the better your skills become. And the more you write your prayers to God, the closer you will draw to Him.

"The closer I draw to God's heartbeat,
the more I realize I need Him."
—Andrew Murray, pastor and author (1828-1917)

Is the Lord Your Shepherd?

The Lord is my shepherd; I shall not want.
He maketh me to lie down in green pastures;
He leadeth me beside the still waters. He restoreth my soul;
He leadeth me in the paths of righteousness for His name's
    sake.
Yea, though I walk through the valley of the shadow of
death, I will fear no evil; for Thou art with me; Thy rod and
Thy staff, they comfort me.

                                        —Psalm 23:1-4 (NKJV)

In her book, Journaling as a Spiritual Practice: Encountering God *through Attentive Writing,* author Helen Cepero writes, "All spiritual disciplines and practices, including journaling, are about learning to be aware and awake, open to God, ourselves, and the world around us. Journaling is meant to give clarity to your day and rest to your night, reminding you even when you are not writing in your journal that God is there with you, in and through it all."

Putting your thoughts, your fears, your joys, your dreams, and your disappointments down on paper is a way to see what is happening in your life. While you can see what is going on around you, it is more important to understand what is happening internally—in your heart, in your mind, in your spirit—especially in response to people and events. When we can grasp that what goes on outside of us has a direct impact on our internal lives, we can better understand what God wants to do in us and through us. Instead of just going through the motions of daily life, we become aware of His presence.

Dr. Bernice Johnson Reagon, a scholar, teacher and songwriter, once said, "Life's challenges are not supposed to paralyze you; they're supposed to help you discover who you are." Reagon grew up in Albany, Georgia, where she became involved in the civil rights movement. In 1961, as a student at Albany State College, she was arrested for participating in a nonviolent student demonstration. Reagon, the daughter of a Baptist minister, spent the night in jail singing songs. After her arrest, she joined the Student Nonviolent Coordinating Committee Freedom Singers to employ music as a tool for civic action. As a songwriter using words to impact others, she has made a difference in this world.

When you use your journal as a tool for discovering who you are in Christ, the world opens to new possibilities and life's challenges lend themselves as experiences for growth. The true goal is a deeper relationship with Him. He created us in His image. Therefore, by knowing God, we come to a better understanding of who we are, whose we are, and what God wants us to do.

> So God created mankind in his own image,
>   in the image of God he created them;
>   male and female he created them.
>   —Genesis 1:27

For most of my life, I could not have told you who the real Carol was; I didn't know myself. If you had asked me, I would have told you whose earthly daughter I was and the name they gave me at birth. I married young, at nineteen, and could have told you that for twenty-eight years I was a wife, before my marriage ended. I am also a mother to two grown sons and a grandmother to five beautiful grandchildren. Before I retired in 2005, I would also have defined myself as Carol Round, high school teacher. However, it wasn't until ten years ago, when I sat down with pen in hand and began to pour out my heart to Jesus, that the idea of who I thought I was began to unravel on the white pages of my journal. During this process of inviting God into my writing, I discovered that my life had been a lie. As a people-pleaser, I had lived life for others and not for Him.

When I recognized the truth that I had not allowed Jesus to be my shepherd, my life's focus and purpose began to change. For me, it was a time for self-reflection, a time to slow down and re-evaluate my priorities. As I did, I began to see God's fingerprints in my life and in the lives of others. I began to see myself as one of His sheep.

> Come, let us bow down in worship,
>   let us kneel before the Lord our Maker;
> for he is our God
>   and we are the people of his pasture,
>   the flock under his care.
> Today, if only you would hear his voice . . ."
>
> —Psalm 95:6-7

Are you ready to hear His voice? Is the Lord your shepherd as well as your Savior?

Writing through the Pain

"I cried out to God for help; I cried out to God to hear me.
When I was in distress, I sought the Lord" (Psalm 77:1-2).

Have you ever felt God has forgotten you? You are not alone. There have been times in my life when I have felt so empty and alone, I have cried out for my Lord to bring me home. I was in so much emotional pain, I didn't want to live.

Marilyn Meberg, Christian author, speaker, and team-member of the Women of Faith organization, has this to say: "I find it wonderfully liberating to talk to God with my humanness showing in all its unattractiveness and not have to worry about what is best for Him. God is the strong one and not I. He doesn't need my diplomacy, and neither does He fall off His throne when I tell what He already knows about my feelings—even when that feeling is anger."

What if we turned to God when we were angry, instead of lashing out at those we love the most? What if we used the blank pages of a journal to pour out our ragged emotions to the One who loves us in spite of our faults? What if we sought God and His forgiveness, instead of harboring negative emotions, which can destroy our peace of mind as well as our health?

God always knows what we are going through. He knows every hair on our heads because He has numbered them. We are significant in His eyes. Why shouldn't we express our pain, our bitterness, our anger, our fears and our inability to forgive to the One who created us, to the One who gave His only Son so that we might be forgiven?

In Psalm 69, David does not repress his feelings when he calls out to God:

> Save me, O God,
>   for the waters have come up to my neck.
> I sink in the miry depths,
>   where there is no foothold.
> I have come into the deep waters;
>   the floods engulf me.
> I am worn out calling for help;
>   my throat is parched.

How often, in our pride, do we refuse to call out for Him? Why do we think we can find the solutions to our own problems? In the process of journaling, we find a safe place to process our thoughts and feelings, a time of discovery, and a way to release deep-seated feelings we may not even have been aware of harboring.

One key to successfully healing from past hurts and disappointments is to keep on journaling, thus letting your heavenly Father inside your soul. He is your restorer. He is your deliverer. He is your healer. In Psalm 37:23-24, David says,

> The Lord makes firm the steps
> of the one who delights in him;
> though he may stumble, he will not fall,
> for the Lord upholds him with his hand.

Pouring out your pain in writing is therapeutic. When you're going through personal stress or anxiety, the act of putting your thoughts in writing brings calm. Instead of staying focused on your grief, disappointment or concern, you become aware of how you're really feeling about the pain. Putting your experience in writing allows you to look at yourself in the mirror of the printed word.

Anyone dealing with a traumatic or emotionally challenging situation can recover from pain and regain a sense of peace. Through the power of journaling, you can feel heard and acknowledged. By regaining your perspective, you feel more in control of the events that have been controlling you.

Most of us carry around something painful. With heavy hearts, we mourn the loss of a loved one, the loss of a relationship, the loss of a job, the loss of innocence, the loss of peace; the list goes on. We all deal with loss at one time or another in our lives. However, we don't have to let it dictate our lives. When we can put in writing what is troubling us, we turn feelings into something real and tangible. In Psalm 69, King David writes:

> Answer me, Lord, out of the goodness of your love;
>> in your great mercy turn to me.
> Do not hide your face from your servant;
>> answer me quickly, for I am in trouble.
> Come near and rescue me;
>> deliver me because of my foes.

Honesty and introspection in your journal opens doorways to healing. In her book, *Writing as a Way of Healing,* author Louise DeSalvo offers this advice:"Write instead of suffering wordlessly."Why should we suffer in silence when we have a God who is bigger than our pain?

We all go through storms in life. Usually we are not prepared, and in some instances, those storms can change the direction of our lives. Uncertainty can be a plague as were the flies that struck Egypt when Pharaoh refused to free the Israelite slaves. During these periods, when our world seems to crash in around us, we can turn to God's Word for comfort and strength.

In Psalm 88, the writer pours out his pain:

> Lord, you are the God who saves me;
>> day and night I cry out to you.
> May my prayer come before you;
>> turn your ear to my cry.
> I am overwhelmed with troubles
>> and my life draws near to death.
> I am counted among those who go down to the pit;
>> I am like one without strength.

I am set apart with the dead,
    like the slain who lie in the grave,
whom you remember no more,
    who are cut off from your care.
You have put me in the lowest pit,
    in the darkest depths.
Your wrath lies heavily on me;
    you have overwhelmed me with all your waves.
You have taken from me my closest friends
    and have made me repulsive to them.
I am confined and cannot escape;
    my eyes are dim with grief.
I call to you, Lord, every day;
    I spread out my hands to you.
Do you show your wonders to the dead?
    Do their spirits rise up and praise you?
Is your love declared in the grave,
    your faithfulness in Destruction?
Are your wonders known in the place of darkness,
    or your righteous deeds in the land of oblivion?
But I cry to you for help, Lord;
    in the morning my prayer comes before you.
Why, Lord, do you reject me
    and hide your face from me?
From my youth I have suffered and been close to death;
    I have borne your terrors and am in despair.
Your wrath has swept over me;
    your terrors have destroyed me.
All day long they surround me like a flood;
    they have completely engulfed me.
You have taken from me friend and neighbor—
    darkness is my closest friend.

If you feel like your only friend is the darkness, think again. God is waiting to comfort you. In his book, *Spiritual Journaling: God's Whispers in Daily Living*, author Dan Kenneth Phillips writes, "Writing in my journal about the storms can be difficult. I often write on the flyleaf of my journals that 'a journal is a place to wrestle with angels and struggle with demons.'"

Struggling through a storm can leave you limping like Jacob after he wrestled with God. Genesis 32 tells of Jacob's nightlong match.

> So Jacob was left alone, and a man wrestled with him till daybreak. When the man saw that he could not overpower him, he touched the socket of Jacob's hip so that his hip was wrenched as he wrestled with the man. Then the man said, "Let me go, for it is daybreak."
>
> But Jacob replied, "I will not let you go unless you bless me."
>
> The man asked him, "What is your name?"
>
> "Jacob," he answered.
>
> Then the man said, "Your name will no longer be Jacob, but Israel, because you have struggled with God and with humans and have overcome."

In our journals, like Jacob, we can wrestle with God, pouring out our pain in ink. We can struggle, but He will help us to overcome. What storms are you going through?

If you're not quite sure where to start, here are some questions for reflection to help jumpstart your healing through writing:

- What have you lost in your past that might still be haunting you?
- Where are your broken places?
- Consider the things you miss or are reluctant to give up. For example: a person(s), a place, a home, a job, a part of your identity, a physical capability, your youth, your innocence, etc.
- What hopes, fears, and dreams are associated with your loss(es)?
- What is your connection to this loss?
- How is this loss connected to others in your life?
- How have these losses affected your ability to move forward in life?
- How have your losses affected your relationship with God?

- Have you asked for forgiveness?
- Did you accept God's forgiveness and forgive yourself?
- How can you nurture yourself towards wholeness?
- What changes do you need to make in your life to get past these losses?
- What is holding you back from letting go of the pain?
- Why do you think God wants you to heal?
- What do you have to look forward to in the future if you can deal with your past?
- What is the first step you need to take in the process of allowing God to heal the broken places?
- What have you discovered about your loss(es) by putting them in writing?

Begin your journaling by having a dialogue with Jesus. Share the pain in your life. Tell Him the hurts you are experiencing, just as you would with your best friend. His grace is enough; it's all we need. His strength, made evident in our weakness, can heal any pain.

More Conversations with God

"Each morning let me learn more about your love because I trust you. I come to you in prayer, asking for your guidance" (Psalm 143:8 [CEV]).

Do you remember the two questions Paul asked the Lord on the road to Damascus? Here is the scene in Acts 22:6-10 as revealed by Luke:

> About noon as I came near Damascus, suddenly a bright light from heaven flashed around me. I fell to the ground and heard a voice say to me, 'Saul! Saul! Why do you persecute me?'
> 'Who are you, Lord?' I asked.
> 'I am Jesus of Nazareth, whom you are persecuting,' he replied. My companions saw the light, but they did not understand the voice of him who was speaking to me.'
> 'What shall I do, Lord?' I asked.
> 'Get up,' the Lord said, 'and go into Damascus. There you will be told all that you have been assigned to do.'

Can you imagine how frightened Paul, known as Saul at the time, must have been when he heard the booming voice of the Lord asking, "Why do you persecute me?"

If you recall, Saul had been a Pharisee persecuting Christian Jews. Now, he was about to become an instrument to spread the Good News. Paul's first question, "Who are you, Lord?" is a question we need to ask. If we truly desire to deepen our relationship with the Creator, we should thirst to know who He is. Paul's second question, "What shall I do, Lord," should be one we ask as well. Through the power of reading scripture, praying, and journaling, God will reveal Himself to you as well as what He wants you to do.

While I grew up in the church, I never asked these questions until my twenty-eight-year marriage ended. I was lost. I didn't know who I was, let alone who God really is. I was merely a church attendee and one who led or participated in activities. I didn't truly know God or that he wanted to have a personal relationship with me.

My prayer life was stale, almost nonexistent. Practicing only rote prayers I had learned as a child, I never knew God desired more for me. However, authentic prayer is as essential to knowing God and growing spiritually as breathing and food are to living. Just as effective communication is important to understanding between an employee and the employer, or between spouses, your relationship with God is only as strong as the conversations between you and Him.

To know God we must seek Him. Jeremiah 29:13 says, "And you will seek Me and find Me, when you search for Me with all your heart." Have you been searching for God with all your heart?

Here are scriptures and suggested responses to contemplate as you continue your conversations with God. Use them to jumpstart your journal conversations, especially if you are struggling with knowing Him.

> "If you . . . search . . . as for hidden treasures; then you will . . . find the knowledge of God."
>
> —Proverbs 2:4-5 (ESV)

How do I find those hidden treasures in your Word? Please help me, Father.

> "Ask, and it will be given to you; seek, and you will find; knock, and it will be opened to you."
>
> —Matthew 7:7 (NKJV)

I'm knocking, Lord. I'm seeking you, Abba. Hear me, please.

"But without faith it is impossible to please Him, for he who comes to God must believe that He is, and that He is a rewarder of those who diligently seek Him."

—Hebrews 11:6 (NKJV)

Help my unbelief, Father. I seek your face.

"I love those who love me. Those eagerly looking for me will find me."

—Proverbs 8:17 (GW)

I love you, Lord. I know you love me too. I want to know you.

"The Lord is good to those who wait for Him, to the soul who seeks Him."

—Lamentations 3:25 (ESV)

I am waiting patiently, Father. My soul seeks You, and only You. I want to know You better.

"And He has made from one blood every nation of men … so that they should seek the Lord, in the hope that they might grope for Him and find Him, though He is not far from each one of us."

—Acts 17:26a-27 (DARBY)

Sometimes, Father, you feel so far away. I want to feel your presence.

"The Lord is near to all who call upon Him, to all who call upon Him in truth."

—Psalm 145:18 (ESV)

I am calling on You, Abba Father. Please reveal Your truth to me.

When you come before God, giving your fears and anxieties to Him, you will receive His peace and comfort. While that doesn't necessarily mean He will take away whatever is causing your worry, you can rest in Him, knowing He is with you and helping you persevere.

As part of your journey, find other scriptures that speak to your needs at this time. Write them in your journal. Ask God to show you how they apply to your life or your situation and how He wants to use them to help you grow.

For more help locating scriptures, use a concordance, an alphabetical listing of words and phrases found in the Bible, showing where the terms occur throughout all the books of scripture.

"Prayer is the breath of the newborn soul, and there can be no Christian life without it."
—Rowland Hill, popular English preacher (1744–1833)

The Pen of a Ready Writer

"My heart is overflowing with a good theme; I recite my composition concerning the King; My tongue is the pen of a ready writer" (Psalm 45:1 [NKJV]).

Just as there is no one right way to pray, there is really no right way to keep a prayer journal. It is a matter of preference. Just as some people prefer kneeling to pray, others choose to sit comfortably in a chair and have a chat with God.

In addition to your Bible, and a daily devotional if you use one, you need a book to use as your prayer journal. Here are some ideas:

- A simple spiral notebook, any size.
- A three-ring binder, which allows you to punch holes in materials that you might want to include for your spiritual growth. (Many devotionals that I receive via email include questions to ask yourself after the devotional reading. These questions can inspire your daily conversation with God. I like the devotions found in *The Upper Room*, *Encouragement for Today*, and *Girlfriends in God*. The latter two devotionals, found online, can be received through email subscription. Any Christian devotional that speaks to you is great for this purpose, but not a requirement.)
- A bound book designed specifically for journaling; they are sturdier and last longer than others. You can also purchase journals designed specifically for spiritual growth. Some include inspirational quotes and writings from best-selling authors, as well as scripture, which can be your guidance for that day's entry.

- If you enjoy scrapbooking or if you are a creative person, you can take a plain notebook and embellish it to reflect your personality. You can add photos, scripture, etc. to make a lively book that you just can't wait to pick up to begin journaling with Jesus.

You also need your favorite writing implement. Like most writers who love the feel of a pen in their hands, I have a variety of ink pens. I don't let the color influence me. Some days I grab one out of the many containers I keep near my chair. Other days, I just grab whatever is handy as I head out to my sun porch to spend time with Jesus. Just like your journal reflects who you are, so does your choice of writing instrument and journaling book. It's a matter of preference.

I know individuals who spend money on bound books of blank pages and fancy pens with their names engraved on them. Personally, I don't spend much on my writing tools. I stock up on journals when I see a clearance sale at my favorite Christian bookstore. This spiritual discipline is not about what you use, but about the journey you are on to establish, nurture and continue your journaling process so that it becomes a regular habit. If inexpensive pens and paper please you, don't waste your money on more expensive ones.

If beautiful bound books and fancy fountain pens are appealing, you will still have a wonderful time on your spiritual journey. I am not opposed to leather-bound volumes and fancy ink pens, if you can afford them. Just remember why you are on this wonderful journey: to grow closer to your Abba Father.

One journaling tool I use sometimes is a unique concept by Steve Laswell, founder of Battle Plan for Believers Ministries. His method, *The Journey: A Personal Journal,* uses three different colored pens and a three-ring binder. In his book, *The Journey: Personal notes from the Father,* Steve explains the method of three voices, three pens (black, green and red) which represent "the three voices found in communication with the Triune Godhead."

"It really is quite simple and only requires a little faith to begin," Steve says. "The black pen is your voice to you." This entry in your Journey notebook answers these questions: "What is going on in your world at this time? What's been happening lately?"

Green is "your voice to God." When using this color, says Steve, "you release thanksgiving and praise, ask questions, share your frustrations, disappointments, fears, hopes, dreams and your thoughts to God."

When you pick up the red pen, listen for "God's voice to you," he adds. "This is God, your Father speaking in the first person to you his child in answer to the question: 'Father, what would you like to say to me today?'"

Steve's personal journal method has worked for me, especially through trials when I feel that God is communicating a specific thought to me after I have poured out my heart to Him in writing, or when I have a possible life-changing decision to make. Steve's journal and book are available at *www.battleplanforbelievers.com*.

Whether you choose a simple BIC pen and plain spiral notebook from the drugstore, or purchase a leather-bound book and engraved pen, remember it's about the journey; a journey to draw closer to your heavenly Father and hear His voice. Select your writing tools and get ready for the greatest adventure of your life.

"Prayer isn't some kind of requirement for believers. It is a privilege!"
—Christa Kinde, author of *Contagious Joy*

Preparing to Meet God

From inside the fish Jonah prayed to the Lord his God"
(Jonah 2:16).

Have you ever tried to run from God? I have. And, just like
Jonah, I couldn't escape. After the sailors tossed Jonah overboard as a
sacrifice, God sent a big fish to swallow him. Hidden inside the belly of
the fish for three days and three nights, Jonah finally cried out to God:

> In my distress I called to the Lord, and he answered me.
> From the depths of the grave I called for help, and you
> listened to my cry."
>
> —Jonah 2:2

If you've ever doubted the power of prayer, picture that big fish
vomiting Jonah onto the shore. We can come to God with all our doubts,
fears, guilt, emptiness, insecurities, pain and all the other messy and icky
stuff in our lives, and you know what? He doesn't mind. We don't have
to pretend to be perfect. We don't have to clean up our act before we
come to Him. We just have to be willing to reach out to our heavenly
Father and listen for that still, small voice telling us, "I love you just the
way you are."

Sitting down with your Bible, a daily devotional (if you have one), a
notebook and your favorite writing implement, is a perfect way to start
listening. Steve Laswell, founder of Battle Plan for Believers, says, "Prayer
means to listen much and speak also."

Like many women who keep prayer journals, I prefer the early morning hours for spending time with God. It's a quiet time before life springs into action like a roller coaster with its twists and turns and ups and downs. Starting the day with God helps me to focus on Him and to remember when difficulties do arise, as they will, I can retreat to that peace I found earlier in my day.

Finding the perfect spot to spend time with God, whether inside your house or outdoors, is another matter of preference. I do both. When the weather is nice, I take my prayer journal, Bible, daily devotional and a mug of hot tea, and enjoy the quiet of my sunroom. Even with a thunderstorm raging outside, I find peace, knowing that God is present for our early morning conversation.

Don't worry.

- Don't worry about His showing up. *He will.*
- Don't worry about your doubts. *Be open.*
- Don't worry about how much time you spend. *God's clock is in a different time zone anyway.*
- Don't worry that you might write something that will offend Him. *You can't.*
- Don't worry about punctuation, spelling, complete sentences or anything else your high school English teacher taught you. *God won't whip out a red pen to make a correction.*
- Don't worry if your words are not "religious-sounding." *God knows your heart anyway.*
- Don't worry about thinking of something to say. *Just come with an open mind and heart.*

Just Do It.

- Do offer what you're thinking and feeling to the Lord. *It's a start.*
- Do make it a daily habit to spend time with Him. *As you continue to use prayer journaling to communicate with God, you will find something wonderful happening. You will be more open and honest with Him and with yourself.*

- Do date each journal entry. *When you return to read earlier entries, you will be blessed to see how He has been working in your life and surprised by your own spiritual growth.*
- Do take time to listen to what He is communicating to you. *You'll start looking for signs of divine dialogue in your daily life. You will begin to think less and less about yourself and focus more on the One who has called you into a personal relationship with Him.*
- Do prayer-journal even when you don't feel like it. *The act of sitting down with Bible, pen, and your journal helps you to focus on God instead of what might be troubling you.*
- Do start writing even when you are having trouble concentrating. *The act of writing your prayers down on paper helps you to stay centered in that moment.*
- Do remember it's not about you. *It's about God.*

"Real prayer comes not from gritting our teeth,
but from falling in love."
—Richard J. Foster, Christian theologian

Come as You Are

"Perseverance must finish its work so that you may be mature and complete, not lacking anything" (James 1:4).

Jesus invites us to come as we are. We are each one-of-a-kind, just as our prayer journals are unique to our experiences and personalities. Depending on our different natures, we may be well-organized or we may be able to function in a holy mess. While I have a difficult time with clutter, my focus is on spending time with the Lord. I'm not overly concerned with formulas and methods. However, you do need something to help you stay on track. In another chapter, I mentioned types of journals. Once you have decided on a type, it will dictate your organization.

For example, a spiral notebook and the bound books designed for journaling do not allow for adding anything from another source, unless you paper clip, staple, glue, tape, or just fold it and stick it in between the pages. The latter can lead to losing something of importance if you are not careful. However, remember this: You are bringing your uniqueness before God, and not a formal by-the-rulebook method of spiritual journaling.

Keeping a journal is about spiritual growth. What are your thoughts and feelings about your faith? Without examination, old thoughts and feelings can continue to lead you down the wrong path. However, by clarifying your beliefs and concerns through spiritual journaling, you have the ability to transform your life.

Written words on a page have the power to help you recognize negativity in your life, negativity that may lead to bitterness and resentment. Life will continue to pass you by until you put your heart on paper and release it to God. In the same way we examine our past, we must explore our faith so it does not stagnate.

Do you want an infusion of energy, strength and purpose in your faith life? Then invite your heavenly Father into the journaling process. Have a God-centered conversation with Him. Prayer is the key component, revealing where God is working in your life and then recognizing and following His plan for you. I encourage you to make this journey about your personal relationship with your heavenly Father, and remember it's a matter of the heart.

I invite you to sign "My Covenant with God" on the following page, an agreement to use a prayer journal for the next forty days. This contract is about your willingness to seek more of the Lord. It's about learning to put God at the top of your to-do list and leaving Him there. It's about a daily commitment and learning to "just be" in His presence.

- Do you want to transform your life?
- Are you willing to make the commitment?
- Are you willing to persevere on this journey to spiritual maturity?
- What are you waiting for? Grab your Bible, pen, and a notebook, and begin your journey.

"Too often we spend all of our time seeking God for answers to our problems when what we should be doing is just seeking God."
—Joyce Meyer, Christian author and speaker

My Covenant with God

"Give ear and come to me; listen, that you may live. I will make an everlasting covenant with you, my faithful love promised to David" (Isaiah 55:3).

Dear Abba Father,

I thirst and hunger for more of you. Your Son said, "Man shall not live by bread alone but by every word that proceeds from the mouth of God" (Matthew 4:4). I cannot live by bread alone. It does not satisfy. Instead, Father, I seek your face.

I come to you in my brokenness and pain, in my joy and thanksgiving. I trust you, Father, to heal me and guide me. I will come before you faithfully, each morning. I will call on you, for you are near.

I know, Father, that your thoughts are not my thoughts, nor are your ways my ways. I only desire to draw closer to you. I agree to be transparent before you, Lord. I will come in all my humanness, releasing control and trusting you to reveal yourself to me.

Your Word says that you are the Author of Life, the Creator of my heart, the Lover of my soul and my Savior and Redeemer. Today, Father, I find myself at a crossroads, ready to take that next step in my walk with you. I know I cannot do this in my own strength, but only in yours. I boldly ask you, through the power of your Holy Spirit, to create in me the ability and desire to focus on this new spiritual discipline.

I know you have great plans for me, Father, plans to prosper and not to harm me, plans to give me hope and a future. As I embark on this new journey, I anticipate hearing that still, small voice, leading me into the future you have for me. I am depending on you, Father, to show me your way.

By your grace, Father, I agree to spend the next forty days focused on learning more about you through my prayer journal. I pray that Your Word will not return empty but will accomplish what you desire and achieve your purposes in my life.

Signed ————————————— Date —————————————

"'For I know the plans I have for you,' declares the Lord, 'plans to prosper you and not to harm you, plans to give you hope and a future'" (Jeremiah 29:11).

More Resources for Your Journey

"After he had finished his work, he became the source of eternal salvation for everyone who obeys him" (Hebrews 5:9 [GW]).

Jesus is our source. He suffered. He died. He rose again. He also has a wonderful plan for each of us. Jeremiah 29:11-13 says, "For I know the plans I have for you," declares the Lord, "plans to prosper you and not to harm you, plans to give you hope and a future. Then you will call on me and come and pray to me, and I will listen to you. You will seek me and find me when you seek me with all your heart."

Seek Him. Follow Him. Feel free to check out the following list of journaling resources to help you on your journey:

Websites

- **http://www.journalingarts.com/** This website offers nice journals for sale.
- **http://www.wellwriting.org/** A website that uses writing to promote physical, emotional, and spiritual healing.
- **http://www.journalshelf.com/** Another site where you can purchase beautiful journals.
- **http://www.go-journal.com/** This site offers free journaling resources, as well as a place to purchase other tools.
- **http://www.aboutcreativejournals.com/** A website offering writing prompts and other ideas for your journey. **http://www.inspiration-for-singles.com/** Join this website

for information on Christian journaling for the single person. There is an excellent e-book there as well, called *101 Sadness Busters for Singles.*

- **www.JustaCloudAway.com** Just a Cloud Away is a support website providing garden, craft, and healing scrapbook kits for early pregnancy and infant loss. This is a lovely website to help parents with journaling and to remember the little time they had with their children before they were called home.

- **www.christian.lifejournal.com** A wonderful way for Christians to journal using an inspiring software package that helps organize and prompt daily prayers and journal entries. **http://www.edge.net/~dphillip/Journal.html** This is a spiritual blog by Dan Kenneth Phillips, a leader in spirituality for over four decades. He has led conferences on prayer, spiritual journaling, the spirituality of Thomas Merton, and spiritual development at retreat centers throughout the United States and Canada. **http://www.thechristianmeditator.com/christianjournaling.html** Rhonda Jones, MA, is an author and the creator of the award-winning website, *http://www. thechristianmeditator.com.*

- **http://www.awomansjourney.com/journaling.html** This site offers resources to learn about enriching the mind, heart, and soul through journaling. **http://therapyinphiladelphia. com/selfhelp/tips/keeping_a_spiritual_journal/** This site offers more insight into the use of spiritual journaling for healing.

- **http://a-christ-followers-musings.blogspot.com/p/journal-prompts.html A** great blog with journal prompts.

- **http://www.writetohealth.com/** Journal Writing for Health is dedicated to helping people discover the healing benefits of journal writing.

- **http://journalinglife.com/This is another** website with a plethora of information on keeping different types of journals, including prayer journals.

- **http://luannbudd.com/A** website devoted to Christian journaling with ideas to keep you writing.

Books

- *The Journey: A Personal Journal* by Steve Laswell
- *The Journey: Personal Notes from the Father* by Steve Laswell (TATE Publishing)
- *Love Letters to God: Deeper Intimacy through Written Prayer* by Lynn D. Morrissey (Multnomah Publishers)
- *Writing as a Way of Healing* by Louise DeSalvo (Beacon Press)
- *Journaling as a Spiritual Practice: Encountering God Through Attentive Writing* by Helen Cepero (IVP Books)
- *Spiritual Journaling: God's Whispers in Daily Living* by Dan Kenneth Phillips (O Books, John Hunt)

About the Author

"My purpose is that they may be encouraged in heart and united in love" (Colossians 2:2).

Carol taught high school English and journalism for seventeen years before leaving the classroom to become a library media specialist. After thirty years in secondary education, God led her from Jay, Oklahoma, to Claremore, Oklahoma, where she currently resides. She is the mother of two grown sons, Casey and Clint.

Carol has worn many hats during her lifetime but the one she cherishes the most is that of "Nana" to five beautiful grandchildren: Cheyenne, Brennan, Cash, Leah, and Luke.

Although she has been a freelance writer for major magazines and had essays and stories published in numerous anthologies, her passion is using her writing gift to glorify the Lord. Her weekly faith-based column, *A Matter of Faith,* runs in twelve Oklahoma newspapers and can be read each week at *http://www.thecypresstimes.com/*. You can also subscribe to her weekly column by emailing her at **carolaround@ yahoo.com**.

Carol's weekly column has inspired over 200,000 readers since it first debuted in November 2005. Her articles, now collected and published in two volumes, reflect on everyday experiences to encourage readers to seek a deeper relationship with the Lord. Using simple stories of faith and sometimes humor, Carol helps her readers to see the wonders of living through our Lord, Jesus Christ. Her down-to-earth sharing of real life and her Christian walk are woven into every piece she creates.

Carol launched her blog last spring where readers can find more inspiration in their walk with the Lord. Her blog, *A Matter of Faith*, is at *www.carolaround.com*. She welcomes reader comments and may be reached through email at **carolaround@yahoo.com** or through her blog.

Other Books by Carol

A Matter of Faith

ISBN-10: 0937660450   124 pages $12.95

In this collection of her faith-based columns, Carol Round uses everyday experiences to inspire her readers to seek a deeper relationship with the Lord. Her weekly column is currently available in twelve Oklahoma newspapers and one online publication, *www.thecypresstimes.com.*

Available in paperback and eBook format for Kindle and Nook. Order this title on Amazon.com or Barnes & Noble.com, or from Buoy Up Press at this address: ***http://www.awocbooks.com/book.cfm?b=54&f=d***

Praise for *A Matter of Faith*:

   "Carol's comforting writing style is soothing and her sage advice is enlightening. Each selection draws the reader's attention to things that are really important. She frequently ends her column with an appropriate action (Whom do you need to forgive?) or challenge (Make a difference) for the reader."

—Rebecca Johnson, Amazon Top 10 Book Reviewer

Faith Matters

ISBN-10: 0937660833   124 pages $12.95

Carol Round's weekly faith-based column, "A Matter of Faith," has inspired over 200,000 readers since it first debuted in November 2005.

In this second collection of her columns, she uses everyday experiences to encourage her readers to seek a deeper relationship with the Lord.

Available in paperback and eBook format for Kindle or Nook. Order this title on Amazon.com or Barnes & Noble.com, or from Buoy Up Press at this address: *http://www.awocbooks.com/book.cfm?b=75&f=d*

Praise for *Faith Matters:*
    "Ms. Round has the nice ability to meld Biblical inspiration with everyday humility to see new wonders of living through our Lord, Jesus Christ."
              —Professor Donald Mitchell, Amazon.com Top Reviewer